BLOOD ACCOUNTS

JAMES WM. CHICHETTO

CONTENTS

VOICE PORTRAIT: FANNIE LOU JUDGE, SLAVE

CONFLICT AND RESOLUTION

SILENCE IN A CHILEAN PRISON

Far away from here you turn dark
and crouch alone like a light ray
bent in the water.

The shadows of the iron bars across your head
and through your eyes
drag over the bottom of stones.

Dreams pulled in under your throat
no longer speak.

The guards, dropping out of their chairs,
strike at everything, hitting your lighted
cigarette,
your hands, arms, your hardened face
because you believe too much.

Life is like coral rubble,
and your eyes underneath, chisel-sharp,
pierce the black night.

And that General,
you must kill him with your silence.

Blind Veteran

He can tell where he is by the echo on the lake,
his paddles brushing against the pickerelweed,
the air giving him its own path over the entire
water.
He talks of battle, of those long dead
far beyond the hearing of other ears,
browsing one summer at dawn,
each soldier taking a step forward
till something happened
and across their clothes blood had grown
out of all they had done.

Now he calls out to my aunt at dusk
above the heads of birds, above shore
fowl and land far back into the rocks
and she calls back to him from a small wharf,
she'll holler him back to shore.

THE BATTLE OF GETTYSBURG, 1863

(Account of Chaplain Wm. Corby, C.S.C.)

Emptied wires unmasked hatred through the smoke;
The glitter of surgery clattered with lies.
Shovels like swords reddened the earth
And scattered their fury inside.
I wept watching the birds beat overhead
With their long silences in the sky
Made starker by the cut-off distances
Of soldiers' sharper cries.
A battle is a fearful thing, monstrous, but
Such bloodshed! Such bone stuck and coming loose!
Such scraps of skin eaten by the black air!
One soldier sat punctured in his booth,
His skull riddled with holes.
Another, with a blow, was split open.
A third, ripped apart as if to defeat valor, purpose.
Now the shadows in the stones fold up
And ghosts tip with a jolt of terror,
And vultures in shredded boughs,
Dwindle our presence to error.

WAR RATS

In the bunker rafters, hanging,
Knotted in some dog's guts, crawling,
Down the rats come,
Their tails rising fleshless like stems
To gnaw on God's sons.

The sides of fingers, greying blood –
Chunked together: skin, eyelids, head —
Grow pale
While small mouths tug from the dead
Their hot entrails.

Bits of brain corniced underneath
Float, spread like fauna, like grease
On a puddle
While rats nip away the meat
Of nicked muscle.

AWAKENED BY STONES

A stone apiece, no race can match that.
We'll soon be upon God at death, they say here.
These are the stones that Jacob lay at.
When we meet at death who will be more dead,
                              O women of Moab?
O Death that has not our wings
Whose longest word no one makes into
                    a new language.
Death whose eyes like medals are pinned to
                              different shirts.
Death with its name maintaining such deeds,
        whose lettering howls in God.
Death undistributed.
Death with no feathers, no beating birds,
Nor chains, nor metal industries.
Death with its incense quartered in stone,
  with its bare arrows flightless into the night.
Death whose practice is always of cold night,
Whose bones cover the shapes of air
Whose convenience is never settled
With its guard on a child's head
With its cap of clay sickness.
I've been awakened by stones, stones laid out
In the heart.
Stones bent to the tongue on words, on awful dark.
Stones that climb death. A wreath of eyes.
A replication of quest.

A STONE APIECE

A stone apiece; no race can match that —
A red bristle along the road, an ebb, neap tide,
Abel's enchantment in black
To lure the Red Sea back.
We'll soon be upon God at death, they say here,
The privilege to split the atom—
Though the soul in yellow dust
Is a new soul steeped in trust
Where the Steeple door is shut
And the Lord's hand takes hold of judgment,
Connecting absence with absence,
Light with light, shadow with shadow and light
From the sole of the foot to the head.
When we meet at death, who will be more dead,
                    O women of Moab,
Bashed by the East wind sprung up,
The wind of many minds sniffed out, many hearts
                    bruised and stricken,
The wind that Uriel screened, curtained under
                    slanting smoke,
The wind of a pile of seeds slumped up against
        wounds, a revelation, a mother-root Epoch
                    of war-tormented sons?
Maranatha, they cry. Come, Lord!
LOVE wrestles the heart to reach the Foe
That ranks with grief and other woes,
The dread of judgment in the soul.

SOLDIERS SHIFT FROM SIDE TO SIDE

Don't separate the dead,
Farmers, plowmen, tradesmen!
Sink them in balm—
Stale eyes, broken heads
Bathed in army lead.

Don't separate the dead,
Black, white or red,
The ranks of brethren –
Guts balled-up in a ditch,
War the color of this.

Safe in their coffins
Soldiers shift from side to side
To share each other dark –
The rage of Job
God's breath blew back
As if against the cold.

EMILY DICKINSON'S CURCUMFERENCE

Meet Emily Dickinson
Guarding our raptures
Where Light appears
In dust-heavy tears.

Centuries cross her hills,
Decades, on two knees;
Years drop from clocks
Like landless leaves.

Time is put on hold:
There fastened to God's dark
With ropes too deep to measure
Our solitude of fact.

Her lyrics ring each distance
Like fences, if you wish,
For Lincoln's grand emotions
And Peter's sack of fish.

DREAM OF ANNE FRANK

You are still part of us, Anne Frank,
Arched against a string of others, millions of them,
Endless, endless,
Unreeling in the wind?

I have watched you in silence wandering,
Left in the streets of Europe,
Passionate beyond hope,
The whole outline of a girl
Blackened by smoke.

The wild trees are burnt now.
The mind soars,
Soars past smoke, past impervious ceilings erupting
To the surface of smoke, inner and outer smoke,
Past thick tongues and mustached mouths
Lit up in the brain,
Past muttering water dripping from wires
And long lines of victims grafted to silence, to stillness,
To an inward Silence keeping them so.

THINGS AREN'T WHAT THEY SEEM

Love wears alike in us
To regulate our lives,
Love like a thread of ardor,
Frayed out at the sides.

But Midas his daughter into gold spun
And Agamemnon surrendered his
To get for Troy fair winds.
Was love kind to them?

FR. SORIN'S FIRST WINTER AT NOTRE DAME, 1842

Under a snow-crust roof they slept:
Sorin in a cot, the Brothers on the floor,
Wrapped in burlap blankets
On scattered straw.

The ground beneath them was cold,
The soot-stuffed chimney blocked;
A board that served as an altar
Was covered with linen cloth.

Outside, snow filled the trails
And burdened the leafless trees
That stretched to the shadowy lakes
And frozen fields.

Packing their stove with wood
Sorin spoke of the Cross's hope
And of thawing winds ahead
And of woolen coats.

Roused by Hope like spring time air
And the venom of sterile wishes,
He learned that loss was gain
Among these timbered riches.

Voice Portraits: THE DREAM OF NORUMBEGA

(The Native American Problem)

OSCEOLA DREAM

Memories here, almost like gun shot,
Darken the sea-wind.
The palm tops are swaying
Against each other as if from within
That sway, the black drink you drank
Gnashed their limbs.

Captured under a flag of truce, you
Still hang as smoke through the air
Above your headless body,
Creating in us a dream that glares,
A reflection of error.

Your musket, long-dissolved in dust,
Once filled the air with shots
Where slaves worked the sugarcane.
Now the roads in front of us
Bear new names
Marking the ground you lost.

RING IN ME YOUR BELL (The Colonist's Song)

Ring in me your bell, O Lord, the dark bell of
Earth's Song! The embryonic song of birth,
With deeper heartbeats than Adam's first!
Lost in memory am I, within myself,
Following that dark song. And there I
Praise the high road of Settlers, the dark road,
Strange with greater roads running through its
Center, the Future, below the standard sun,
Cosmic high over Eden's ground of trade
And frontier, with stubborn voice resounding!

O America that never stops, whose blessings, deeds
Skid-by brazen, wild, as if in ribbons,
Deeds thick as shadows in a forest, more
Just than Winslow's bullets! I rip a button from
Europe's coat! I rip ten more from it as she
Whips out a gun from some king's belt! And poor Britain
In her star-studded dream, grieving, evanescent!
Now I hold a torch with an axe, face turned
Forward, outward! I walk America, an America
Of Beauty, not past, with each river's ring pealing, its
Suppliant sky gonging, with Settlers heard stirring
With nothing but the Future nearby, at large, ahead,
And the clatter of wheels clapping them forward!

HERE YOUR HEARTS BURNED

(The Natives' Complaint)
Here your hearts burned like a torch to answer
Europe's brand, its counsel for discovery, revelation,
Knowing to tame a people, to subdue them to
A King, you needed first to prop up his will;
Here you made your stations operative
By the way in which you worked them,
Treading on the heels of some, slaughtering
Others; learning to deal with yourselves
For greater conflicts to come. In this you grew,
Expanded, grew large to ferment evil, exploit good.
O there was so much to flee from your harsh spell!
The plague and tease of killing!
Surely, Hispaniola was calamitous,
The uprooting of the Tiano, their
Extermination mourned by Friar
Bartolome: disease and torment in
Labor, watery food from black crops;
Abandoned villages bathed in rotting
Flesh; the froth of illness and gun-blast;
Bitter rivalries cohering without fragile
Justice or respect; and gross, vexatious greed.
We were stripped to the soul, laid low by you,
Quartered to make your sons rich.

BUT EUROPE'S DIET

And Europe's diet turned to good account,
Improving with rice, maize, and potatoes,
Enticing thousands to seek relief by
Immigration to lighten their burdens.
The route to foreign lands would prove gainful
To Englishmen, Scots, and Welsh beneath the
West Wind's Breath. Mouths would no longer pine
For food in tight-lipped silence; the handclasp of
Fortune would purge age-old needs from
Britain as she lengthened her shadow on
Norumbega and the South. And as men
Began their march to cut the earth with trenches
And drains, with impressions and lines, their
Weeds and rats, their pathogens like ravenous
Fiends called into view a fresher prospect,
A bolder landscape for pigs and cattle,
For goats and sheep, horses and oxen,
Cotton and tobacco. Soon forests glistened with
Axes as men hacked down trees for lumber,
And leveled forests for new, reaching farms
That closed us out.

THIS WE WITNESSED

This we witnessed, the horror amidst epidemics that
Left flesh in heaps for flies to pick, and frenzied
Maggots swelling like yellowed sores on which
The Conquest shone. These bore the dreaded
Seal of death in village cribs and wigwams,
Bulging in their season's heat as if to swell
Paradise with rot and embroidered bones.
No more would villages be dense with Native
Peoples as pathogens old bred new ones:
Smallpox, measles, typhus – as if these plagues
Were nothing new, only inevitable rudiments,
Germs before a frost or lagging sun.
Soon elders died and their wisdom along with them,
Quenching in death bewildering truths that
Once passed back and forth among generations.
Then tribes on their knees fell to disruption
As if leveled out of heaven's reach,
As emigrants thickened and enslaved Africans
Cleared the land of empty villages,
Abandoned and fenceless for a new god.

COULD CAESAR DO BETTER?

Could Caesar do better, entreats Squanto,
Raising imperial stones?
And what of Alexander,
Ground to dust and bones?
These forged Glory for the truth
Under Plato's ceiling;
Made a cave a single glacier
And the Law, a woman kneeling.

Whatever you smear with mud or dirt
Whatever you cloud with smoke
Congeals above the ruins
Of Caesar's painted hope.
Powhatan's song, King James's hymns
Rest in some coat of arms
Rolled up in Caesar's threads,
Packed with flags and guns.

KING PHILIP'S CRY

Tell America's Angels
We haven't been blessed!
Bring out their righteous prayers
Where Massasoit rests!

Mix newness with emblems old,
Mix Roanoke's daybreak with bleach!
Come raise the skies of America
That the Eagles reach!

Explain the Algonquin sky,
Powhatan's ebon feathers
Whose vengeance caresses blood
And smears the Northern weather.

Slow, slow the hammer beats
Refining Powhatan's land
With a candle in John Smith's head
And a red glow on his hand.

WEETAMOO'S REPUKE

Awake, you Dukes of York!
Prevail upon your king!
His crown shrouds a liquor barrel
That maddens the sexton's ring!

Free Yoruba slaves
With gold to replace the dead
And fur and hides
From some rich trader's bed!

Plunge a knife into Europe's side
Whose streets are clogged in mud!
In Drake's dreams, too large for him,
Plunge your word of blood!

MASSASOIT DREAM

God told Massasoit
To deal with the children of Saul
Inside a wigwam of stars
That menaced and lit his walls.

The hollow air of the night
Encompassed the Pilgrim world
Descending from the Mayflower
Against the English word.

God said He'll nail one sachem
To the trunk of Plymouth's wood,
Nailing his feet and bones
On a hill where robbers stood.

Then He put his hands
On a monster's face
On the black dust of a room
Where the Pilgrims ate.

Part of His message went dead
Among women and others
And among warriors out of the past
Who raided their brothers.

Now we're left with Hecuba again
Piling Hector's arrows among stones
And Metacomet's majestic head
On the detritus of English bones.

MASSASOIT'S EPILOGUE

1.

Virginia, be at peace!
There is no boiling pot to stir;
The odor of war and blood
Was cleared for ampler air.
Leave John Smith and Percy
At this epoch's end.

2.

And what of Percy's venture,
Taking a chieftain's wife,
Thrusting a sword through her
For fear she might be right?
What repeal of principle
Reached King James that night?

3.

When Pocahontas died of disease
There were no distant peals or booms;
London redressed no wrongs;
The business of war resumed.
Smith knew these specters of greed
That haunted his room.

VOICE PORTRAIT OF GEORGE WASHINGTON

(on Wars and Slavery)

WASHINGTON ON HIS LIFE

There's no room for lies here
Under the day's sun, nor perch for fools
With grease-fouled tongues!
But brassy I'll start whatever your remarks
As the sun struts over the hill
With the day's good will!
But take not my dare to a whipping post
To labor Job with hope or Judas from despair....
I'm my brother's keeper
But like the peal of thunder!

My claims ought be more modest:
Great grandson of a planter –
Blood-mouthed he, un-puffed, earnest,
A bribe to his betters;
Whose soles on the planks of docks
Stalked fretting as he walked
Long before quitting England
And the balm of that land....
Aye, ranks before me will parade
Piping of him and kin –
Off like the wind in the sun's fat blaze!
To eclipse a Past he came
For an eye-stunned change!

WASHINGTON ON HIS VALOR

I know mine and mine know me,
Chides the Lord in Scripture.
I, too, know such as if in near sleep
Or in dreams saddled to a steed
Of never-ending consciousness
Or in awkward reverence left
To do what I must do!
Something burns true in me, and pure, something
Rough-cast I seize upon with both hands
Knowing right friends will stand
By me year after year,
Vigilant, watchful with iron wills.

Such are my thoughts some days,
As if on a cusp of surety,
Thinking past hot-blood dreams, war scores,
Or steps of a maid toward me.
I know the risks at times like this –
The perils one takes
To dot a victory, leap too quickly!
But when battles have drops
Worse than feet can reach,
Depths where demons meet,
I cloak with Wisdom my thoughts
For sure Providence and cold sense!

WASHINGTON GRIEVING HIS BROTHER

But travel's useless! He is dying!
No wave-deafening air can rouse him,
Make him less ill, nor island check his end.
Later in Bermuda he dies, dies –
Is shut off with those spirits in that Last Great Silence!
O Lord, God, to what is best in me he spoke
To lure a better hope.
He was ever my counselor, mentor, father,
Fixed on my future, that sphere and quarter
To expand, to strive for, and find
Deep within the mind.

But what an autumn! Appalling still
As if lengthened under grief
That I hasten to!
Yet the years chastened leap!
When spirits lie beaten
They lie not dead but rave at will
As if reaching through steel,
To gain hold of the punished living.
But excess of grief the speedy brain impedes.
What more can I do as surveyor
I'll face as soldier.

WASHINGTON ON BEARING ARMS

But frightened, held back? I know my weakness
Having given face to war; yet know, too, the unrest
To bear no arms the more.
I need no fiddling recruiter
To injure my soul.
I know already my choice
As if overhearing a ghosted voice.
So in no time I stand dressed, ordering
A new uniform with gold loops and hat adorned
As if tailor-best.
What was once dear to me is ever dearer to be:
To bear arms as soldier
However much blood's on one's coat fir
Or boots worn or toes swelled with corns!
Even in sleep I thing this
With each brewed myth I conjure up –
However, rated with buttons shiny—
As though a great shadow of fate on the wall
Can glimpse apace my ruin.
But in the night's coolness before rest
I know I'm blessed.

WASHINGTON ON BRADDOCK'S DEFEAT (I)

And poor General Braddock, felled
By a bullet gashing his arm,
His noble lung, goring!
His spirit at once strong, so strong as if ahead
Of him, compassed on that bloody field,
But desperate in struggle, feeling a kind of fury
Surface, stripping his victory first, then leaving
Him little hope. I was to carry out his orders –
Relay a message to Dunbar for supplies,
Pound the route back on horseback for hours
Through blood-dark horror.

And horror it was, with shocking scenes of
Corpses rotting or rotted. And the watchful cries
Of the maimed and dying not yet gathered.
O what a flesh-hacked scene to flee heightened
To shreds in me as if holding captive within the
Murderous day a blood-shrunk night.
O the groans I heard and lamentations
Of men struck down on skull-wrecked ground,
Lost faces to lost names!
Sleepless I rode from that defeat,
Grieving as rage and disgust broke sleep.

BRADDOCK'S DEFEAT (II)

Later, Braddock dying, two miles
From the Great Meadows,
Hands me a sash and two pistols.
I feel the rush and flow of temper, his look,
His racked face as if hacked off, disgraced,
His chest half-bared, his sweat-splattered hair
Reared in idiot fashion as one not of a great army
Or regimental breed but as Crassus brought down!

He was beaten by his own, a trifling hem of men,
Cowardly blood-swollen regulars, languishing,
Weak-kneed, ghastly! Who would have thought it?
Regulars devoid of grit, of nerve, who practiced
Hard in their land to chase foxes than men!
I oversaw the burial that no impious foot
Or savage triumph would stir his peace
Or maul his laurel. I let no music stand;
Only prayer for a great man!

BRADDOCK'S DEFEAT (III)

A trench we dug in the road for his body,
Blanket-wrapped; lowered it cold near the
Site mapped. We stood round in prayer.
The torch-light larger (giving vague dimensions
To the men) seemed to light up our words
Grown sad and small as though God was all
And we his half-lit world.
Then we moved on, run by events
And rush for profit.

Such scenes make one think again and again
Of our boisterous hope, its engine germ,
The source of our land, the rudiment hands
That plough it and till, work at what they will
As if for greater dreams
Before some cold sun dips and age sits
Raveled in those fated to leave,
Not adverse, however much the years trot
To slack our surge-driven lot!

Washington and his Slaves (1)

And what have I of slaves
To keep them reckoned, bound here —
But for good rule and will,
My rigor, discipline to steer
Them as if to mightier tasks
Under days that pass!
They are my people, half-defined,
Come to labor with me! But I sell them as any
Planter and score with ready profit when
They are fat and lusty, with nimble limbs sounder;
Though under a servitude broad, each thrall I singly rule.

On Sundays, they are foot-loose, free to take on the ready
Yield of crops, loaded to the ear! Unbridled, free
To cede reserves, sell stock, till gardens, turn upwards as if
To face the pendent sun or a preying bird; examine
What they will of grass, of buzzing flies that sail,
Hum from toe to head,
Scud swill or land on some stool or plank-bed.
My slaves are free of flogging, small pox,
Penalties rarest made to shock!

But what of release, liberty, replete with troubles
That our system breeds?
Must we flout heaven with shackles,
Heedless of David, the Hebrew king?
And who are we to rid, dispatch bondage, evil
When to live here is hopeless
Without their harnessed juice –

Though we know ourselves our customs wrong,
Our ill-stared justice given to questions amiss,
Frail offense, as if cocked to rush inevitable Doom!

WASHINGTON AND HIS SLAVES (2)

Has soul answer to this error
Given how its darkness crawls,
Grows utmost as if to the point of cure,
Intolerable to all?
Have we only vague assurance
Of some cryptic date we advance
In mind or soul? Some tomorrow half-born,
Routed again and again
As if to hold back life to come
And what freemen ought
Feel? Have we this scourge until we adopt,
Vouch from within that all are one –
That liberty be sanctioned, passed on
And bondage wrong?
One's past is strong all the more
Like any past of life that is no more
Except for whom the past
Has failed free men. But our past
Conferred wealth, might;
We were reared on that labor,
That reasonable error,
Whose soldered wounds shall never heal,
'tis said, however folks are patient,
Schooled in sense, slow in degrees to zeal.
But for now, we are lost
As shackled limbs reap crops.

WASHINGTON'S CRY AGAINST THE BRITISH AND HIS CONCERNS

No! Nothing stands still
To any happening! Nothing!
Every moment is the right one
To make just the law
And what we have left of freedom!
Our foes shall only strengthen us –
Our excellence, our stealth –
Where blows are hardest, most severe;
And when out with lanterns ahead of them,
We shall date them with their deaths.

Yet I lament at times such hubbub stress,
Such inventions of war and method
Down to the populace
Like the mutinous turns of shafts and wheels
Of an engine,
As if making Rule fall and rise at whim,
Making heedful its spin, and necessary
And contrivance free.
We break so much inside
Our bidden worlds, our plough-marked order
As if to create a people better
Whose outcome's but a civic sign,
A mirror as if to proceed with double caution
However the perversion wrong.

WASHINGTON ON THE AMERICAN REVOLT (1)

A brother's sword is sheathed
In a kinsman's breast;
Peace is cold, bleak
As if choked, adrift.
Fields are bared.
The windows of Boston,
Blacked out, numb.
Hate creeps into a neighbor's yard—
One a Tory, the other patriot.
Anger outstrips thought.
Even the sky is hard.
Muskets bleat out the hate of men
Or rage begun.
But unity must be most upper
Amongst us; no irresolution
Ought tilt us from one side or the other
To addle action.
I believe Gates and Lee
Catch in me
Less than they look for,
Yet cling as if to my grade in fear.
Or loyalty, they are bustling born,
But of self-interest more,
Deeming victories for sure
Belong to them o'er me.
But I live with such poison
And swap it, strengthened.

Washington on Benedict Arnold

But we never catch him!
I send spies, assassins
To New York, culled men
Bid to kill him.
But he escapes anew –
His leprous flight
Over ready waves with British knaves!
Be gone, cur! Be gone, traitor,
White-faced captain to your country men!
Be gone from this home,
Its settled peace, its ruddy splendor!
Never come back, never, never
To enter the realm of soldier!

The rot is ever here of traitors,
Perfidious fiends reared in malice
Past sleep, terror! Their Judas-chore
Awakens stress,
Edgy affliction, distrust,
Adversities they suck best —
These rat-shadows, bloody
For money!
So many betray, lie
Awake to ensnare, beguile a country
To despoil what they see
'Ere they evilly die.
Arnold was no less, no more than one
Monstrous fiend of Adam!

AMERICAN REVOLUTION (2)

When Congress takes charge of Boston,
Its troops in Roxbury,
I'm loud as a wind's roar
To include me.
Men sharpen their knives, hug wives
Knowing to more fiery ventures they'll be sent
As if to annul bondage, shatter it, rend its maggot-rope
In rage. These events I follow as if to Himalaya go.
Bunker Hill's a victory of sorts
For hare-eyed Brits. They count
A thousand dead and reflect on the carnage,
The slaughter, turning over dead men on their backs—
The price of their attack.
That evening, with lanterns lit, Howe knows the triumph
Was a palm too costly!
His boots, blood-soaked, wadding Victory,
Had smothered it.
I am off to Cambridge to assume the role I sought.

CROSSING THE DELAWARE RIVER

Cold, cold was that crossing—
Bitter, bitter that winter chill coming
Against the glare of men,
Field-stripped and thin.
What went wrong in Manhattan?
At the heights, at Harlem?
At Chatterton's Hill, at Fort Washington?
No need to crouch idly as if over a map. I was there!
My expertize useless to me
As if only to breathe in the air en route to the Delaware!
But I'll avenge this black event!

AMERICAN REVOLUTION (3)

And the arrogance of them! On our rivers
Increasing our numbers dead!
Are we to squat in horror,
Fold hands, shrink, cower, bow heads
As they guest-cover the earth,
Fill with music our curse?
Damn them repairing our ready forts
As if to keep them ripe for Court and King!
I'll not long become feeble to this,
Breaking ice to bits, on the run!
I'll route this defeat or swell a madness deep!

Poor Turlygod, poor Tom,
Out of his mind today!
His butcher friend gone,
Drowned in clay
The Tories say!

When the sun comes up
For the vomit-mouthed with smallpox,
The sun is hot!
And blood's on a flagpole
From soldiers shot!

WASHNGTON AT VALLEY FORGE

I to myself prate, talk, speak as if to not myself outsmart
Or cull conceit with a maimed heart.
But the Forge – how stark, that Valley at every moment
More stark, worse for virtue, food, mercy,
Turning minds to frenzy! How does one liken hunger
To raw savagery? Or both to cruelty? Which is fiercer,
More violent? From Cain downward we discover
All stand ruthless to savage hunger.

But camp we set up as best we could after Morristown
After Brandywine, Burgoyne's defeat to shut things down!
What else had I to do with dysentery afoot, typhus, scurvy,
With men devoid of soap, shoes, made worse by bad news!
For want of blankets they froze,
Their minds turning inward, whirling towards victory,
A warm cot, or what they chose.
My ground was slipping and all beneath me to hell.

Was that not pain enough, agony? What more for America?
What more? But we rose from disorder, edged by discipline
With von Steuben's arm of effort – the fires he roused best
To duplicate and redouble with will
What victory feels! "Give me time," he tells me, "One glimpse
Of hope a day; I'm closer to victory than Caesar displayed."
Then I knew Providence would hustle this cause
Or from this end toss us!

THE COMING OF THE FRENCH, YORKTOWN, 1781

Then that Penury that plagued mind and heart
Is no more! NO MORE! As if on a ledge
I stood. The sea pulsed, my doubts ripped to shreds!
Rochambeau and de Grasse make us visible, real!
I strip fear to the skin, rip out its carcass-lining, its
Inner dread, never to load my head! Coy Cornwallis
Waited for his reinforcements. Clinton hedged.
They fought in redoubts, spiking cannons, guns,
Shuffling, lunging forward to withdraw from
Trenches, empty them out, run!

Then the fields
Fell silent and a flag flapped white.
The toll of that victory: Fields paved with bodies,
Black and white, a grave of one vast smell, with arms
Sticking up and rotting limbs like giant plants to fill hell;
War's dark-light of terror with creaking barrows rutting
The limp earth to sweep fields clean! Cornwallis's
Deputy presents his sword. He couldn't himself,
So contemptuous of me! Lincoln, my deputy, accepts
It to Yankee Doodle's word. Then it ended!
We sheathed swords, cheered – dirty, ragged, bold!

YORKTOWN, VIRGINIA, 1781

Have you something for these soldiers
Felled at Yorktown,
Wearing the badge of courage
On this stone-dressed ground?

Their absence is left to heaven
Past streets with fading song,
Where not even their graves
Stand firm for long.

They left us to redress a wrong,
A region frosted with light,
In the racked quarters of war
And the emergence of night.

Have you something for these soldiers
To come to terms with them,
Their death for their country
Against the bugler's hymn?

WASHINGTON'S APOLOGY FOR BRAC-ING SLAVERY

This thing of Darkness –
This I acknowledge, divvying me up in darkness!
'Tis never unacknowledged, un-avowed.
But I temper it – the absolute, the arbitrary,
The will over others,
The power to kill at any time –
This I temper!
And our surrender to Silence,
Its dust in a windy street,
Chewing into expunged voices, breasts,
Saw-toothed into ribs, looting lawful hearts,
The slaves' maddened hope!
This I temper!

But what choices had I
Beyond historic law where
Ghosts echo still? Beyond expedience,
The effort to render each his due
As future-seers overlay this show,
This receipt of utility?
But without strength to curb might, Justice is little,
Is but a shot thundered in sleep,
A ghost beckoned, a hapless shade,
Dispersed like smoke into any wind
Without force to second it, abet it,
Stand by it with iron arms
For bondmen, helots, vassals
And wrath to come.

APOLOGY TO FANNIE LOU JUDGE

O what part is never told!
What part is severed, rent wide open –
Ever opening to the rest!
What liable skin of a man's hide
Is beaten still, whip-oppressed
To parading shadows!
You know, I know the spectacle,
What past is never seen,
What sound of treading feet
Trampling, unbidden, alarmed by watchmen
Is never gone! What veiled yoke
Downward into darkness
Is mine still
That seeks an argument, a dispute,
A stranger devil to wound!

O the darkness of it all,
The wantonness,
That I am made, too, a self-dared fool
To enact a blood-ceased moment, a variant future,
A grant to your gift of blood
Where Minutemen stood!

VOICE PORTRAIT: FANNIE LOU JUDGE, SLAVE

FANNIE LOU'S RESPONSE TO GEORGE WASHINGTON

But still headlong nothing! Into nothing! Our desolation,
Blank to you! Our dirt-veined feet on blood-fields,
Blood-oceans! Nothing! Teeth torn out, broken!
Flogged! Salt, fisted into wounds! Nothing!
Names whipped from memory! Limbs cut! Nothing!
You with your gloves of henchmen's cloth!
A face without eyes! Knuckle-white! Nothing!
Blows with a paddle! Sawed off legs! Chopped toes,
Broken backs! Nothing! Salt pork, cornbread rotting!
Blood-blest meat! Maimed, charred torsos, burnt trunks!
Nothing! With your fixed prices like celebrant snouts
Overhead! We face down to stay clear of terror!
Shun horror! The bud out of evil! Darkest crime!
Slave, black — alike death-tag! Nothing!
Nothing! Bloody welts! Soul-trashed, hushed-up
Under lynching trees!

FANNIE LOU ON HISTORY

There's a lot to say of war and battle,
Appointing weight to ventures,
Deeds of one sort or another
Fraught with dangers!
Yet is that what we're about,
To make Thermopylae true,
The sound of picks and shovels
As if gut-wrenching new?
But let's begin
From depths of the past
Where one truth ripens,
Crueler than the last.

Make ready for the clanging!
Fetch the prophet's psalm
For slaves who've ceased to wait
For counterfeit balm!

Can birds resume the egg?
Can men the womb
Or Eden recommence
A divine tune?

Wait an' see, wait an' see!
The Searchlight beam is bright
As musket barrels jerk
And twitch for Light!

FANNIE LOU ON WASHINGTON

Thrifty Washington!
Wadding swamps, dreams, bare-headed! Rigged out in boots,
Sunburnt hope, heavy-eyed to wipe clean the slate, pure
As a knife's heart! That's America, sir, over trenches
Space-rich, over crop and fields sun-cracked on maps
Predestined, with Providence blazing down reticent,
Fir-green! Everything for the taking!

He played as his forefathers played
Abetted by fortune, estate,
Ambition jointed by pain
As farmers spilled the same blood
Bashing Natives' brains.

It was as if all the dead broke into words
When they won at Yorktown,
Their invisible hands beating the earth
As if to hoist on air a curse on England
For their deaths and suffering!

FANNIE LOU ON HOMER

Ever wonder about sage Homer
Who heeded how the Greeks fought,
Whose oars beat deadly against the Waves,
But beat deadlier in their hearts?

His lines pelted the weak and the strong,
His blood-choked words were dark,
Sprawled on a sheep skin scroll
Like blood on a dog's back.

About the measure of men, he wrote,
Whose heroes cut each other's throats!
Hector's dragged behind a chariot
Like a dog on Homer's rope!

Blood looked at Homer like water,
Like every murder,
The flow of Abel's blood.
Nothing could freeze that river
Bronzed by weeds and mud.

FANNIE LOU ON HURT

I'm made out of Words
But Stones are just as hard.
I'm one who greets such Stones
To rate them good or bad.

But must I laud the good today
Or wring dry the bad?
I've known my kitchen feet to trudge
On battlegrounds as hard.

Poor me! I must contend with hate
As in the Bible's past
Where Words are as hard as Stone
To satisfy and last.

Fannie Lou on Conscience

How high's the platform-conscience,
How high the apple tree?
Is it worth a candle flame
In the distance?

O what of Consequence, Sir,
When interiors are cold
And men crack open a skull
For imperial show?

I clap my hands in praise
And fill the sky with song
Whether I face a gallows
Or heart once strong.

But think of that small light
When the General's eye is dead
And evening with its scent
Is black above his head.

FANNIE LOU ON THE EVIL OF SLAVERY

Sin boldly, they say!
But against self or prey?
Against want or deficiency
To swallow up the day?

But what of murder, betrayal,
Some hurt of the mind
When hate eats it up
Or conscience sits blind?

Where does the Master in good stead stand?
Must he adjust again
To Bondage, the hangman's
Curse, as citizen?

"But what of family," he cries,
"and the country's oneness?"
As guilt begs innocence
With cunning breath.

Yet Evil still it is
That freedom doesn't bring
As we trek each Golgotha
Before perishing.

Fannie Lou on Solidarity

We're not alone on this earth
To rot in this den
Where Light's halted like poison
And heaven's stars are tin.

We're not alone in this grief,
To hold Apocalypse back
When the seeds of time are crackling
In a shifting sky of black.

We're not alone in this pit
Like dogs who squirm and stink,
Whose victories are in place
To fit some Planter's speech.

All the while we stand and pray –
Poor wretches are we,
Our chary presence
With our gallantry.

FANNIE LOU ON THE MIDDLE PASSAGE AND THE AMERICAN REVOLT

Sharks look aside each other
Rolling the dead who drowned,
Marked without names or faces
Fathoms down.

Who are these kin cast-off,
Added to the sea,
Sunk down to sleep and death
Too brave for pity?

———————————————

Outside I watch from a Yorktown bunker;
My heart war-wearied reeks.
The bombs I think are thunder;
My breath, Elijah's speech.

A musket cocked to yield a drop
Is all that blood can stop
As ranks of soldiers march
And lead balls leap like frogs
By Degradation's Rock.

FANNIE LOU PRAISING BLACK VETERANS

Now let us praise famous men,
Black men aflame, grown mightier
On battlefields, in struggles doomed,
Who'd breathe their last sigh to fight
Than give Oppression room.

The Redcoats on their shoe-black paths,
The Redcoats beaten down,
Crossed their Hausa guns,
The jingling of their spurs—
Their steeds on Jacob's ground
Heralding the dawn.

Find room in a song for them
In the gong of a bell's din
When Freedom's song if knelled.
The barrel of their musket's still
To gunshot and drill.
Find room in a song for them
Who half-filled hell.

FANNIE LOU ON HOPE

Hope outweighs a Wilderness
When Hagar's pushed away
To bear grief and misery
And notch a better day.

Joseph to good turned malice
When bound in Pharaoh's chains!
He snuffed the smell of his brothers
For wiser change.

FANNIE LOU'S SEVEN CIVIL WAR PROPHESIES : PROPHESY 1

I am no shadowy Prophet of six thousand years ago!
I summon what I see from the shadows of time,
From Degradation to spluttered rhyme!

War flows like a fiery wind here!
That's the Lord's judgment, His redemptive raid,
A fiery breeze that blots the air
To rescind the solder's blade.

O frightened men with war-patched hands,
Pursue a path more ample!
The height of Sinai's stony crest
Where Jacob rests
Rears a blasphemous temple!

Beside a helmet, a soldier,
Reckoning Apocalypse,
Grips an Angel's plume
From Jerusalem
Where every gate is pearl
In a wood-smoked room.

PROPHESY 2

The moon-eyed woman's grief
Is scant in Randolph's mind
Like scraps in heaps about his yard
Or chaff at cutting time!

Angels sift through stricken cities,
With speckled hooks-for-meat.
The corpse of an uneaten body
Lies patient in the street.

Pus spurts from a house slave's eye
Whose clothes smell of blood!
Fury flies to her head!
Can one grudge her rage?

A blow to the head
Where hate abounds!
Are those his lips
Wetting the ground?
O Jesus Lord
Beaten down!

O Moses in my holy mouth,
You shook a king to bits!
My words are Jeremiah's sparks;
Isaiah's off my lips!

PROPHESY 3

I groan, Lord, with the Hebrews,
But prophets may be late.
Cotton grows like silver here
Shot through with iron weights.

Bloodshed trails their hoof-beats
Where Angels drop their wings,
The fiercest of them savage,
The savage of them, kings.

America's baring herself, her Specter,
Where Killing Angels move
To dwindle like a shadow,
A Ghost within a groove.

My prayers step off into heaven
Like travelers in the night.
You are good and forgiving, Lord,
Within this Room of Light.

But men quit their kitchen fires
For Truth and right to tell,
For Losses they can live with
And Abel's right to kill.

PROPHESY 4

By white-washed sheds near beaches
And slave-pens streets away,
He hawked his field-hand chattel
To average out his day.

Now he's dead by daffodils
Where slavers can't be heard,
A well-remembered son
Who scoured the business world.

But big-eyed frogs near-by
Like rats infesting grain
Riot by his stone
On which kin bled his name
And riot by the sod
And muck that feel the same.

PROPHESY 5

Make Peace our trodden path!
Scroll Freedom in the dirt!
Wash vomit from our shackles
With a slaver's shirt!

Age bondage to its death
From London to Cape Hope!
It's beautiful to shout aloud
And drop a Planter's coat!

Who will sink the trader's ship,
The Zong man's whip and rod?
A deacon from the parish says,
When God stops killing God!

She wrote on a Gospel wall,
A wall in Jerusalem!
She wrote on a Wall of Rain
Through which a Wind came!

She cut a Lamb in two,
Sucked blood off its cheek!
From sand below a tide
She raised Elijah's feet!

A wind howls in her soul,
A maelstrom of Three Wraths!
The weight of Yahweh's Word
That rolled an ocean back!

PROPHESY 6

Rejoice not over me, O Masters,
In soap-white suits!
Through I'm in chains, I shall arise
And follow the road to Jerusalem
Whose Judgment is swift and given.

The Lord will take up my cause,
Will fetch me forth to Light
With stripes on my back
And chain-ringed legs,
Above the time-stricken night
Where no need there'll be for passage,
Half-way or middle, or heaving sea,
And Justice shall shine bright!

PROPHESY 7

"And was the holy Lamb of God…seen?

William Blake

The Lamb of God will round a darker blood,
Will turn the knuckles of Achilles' hand
A deeper red
In Jacob's land.

The deer of Isaac will not leap in vain;
The Romans' javelin will stick in sand.
Graves will open to a scorching sun
And dust will close the gun.

Where evils abound,
Who will cancel bondage for the slave?
Piedmont's Laws will be ripped to shreds,
And Planters, stalked like prey.

And all shall be well
And all shall be well in the land!

ACKNOWLEDGEMENTS

Some of the poems in this volume were previously published in various literary magazines, including THE CONNECTICUT POETRY REVIEW, THE COLORADO REVIEW, COMBAT LITERARY JOURNAL, GARGOYLE, PLAINS LITERARY JOURNAL, POEM LITERARY MAGAZINE, AMERICA, ROUGH BEAST, among others.